INVESTIGATE!

HIGH GEAR

PORSCHES

Enslow Publishing

THERESA EMMINIZER

Please visit our website, www.enslow.com.
For a free color catalog of all our high-quality books, call toll free 1-800-398-2504 or fax 1-877-980-4454.

Library of Congress Cataloging-in-Publication Data
Names: Emminizer, Theresa.
Title: Porches / Theresa Emminizer.
Description: New York : Enslow Publishing, 2023. | Series: High Gear | Includes glossary and index.
Identifiers: ISBN 9781978528703 (pbk.) | ISBN 9781978528727 (library bound) | ISBN 9781978528734 (ebook)
Subjects: LCSH: Porsche automobiles–Juvenile literature.
Classification: LCC TL215.P75 E46 2023 | DDC 629.222–dc23

Published in 2023 by
Enslow Publishing
2544 Clinton Street
Buffalo, NY 14224

Portions of this work were originally authored by Seth Kingston and published as *The History of Porsches*. All new material in this edition is authored by Theresa Emminizer.

Designer: Leslie Taylor
Editor: Theresa Emminizer

Photo credits: Cover (car) Darren Brode/Shutterstock.com; Series Art (background swooshes) NAAN/Shutterstock.com; Series Art (sport alphabet) geen graphy/Shutterstock.com; Series Art (banner) Natykach Nataliia/Shutterstock.com; p. 5 Lucille Cottin/Shuttertstock.com; p. 7 GEORGE STAMATIS/Shutterstock.com; p. 9 AGF Srl/Alamy.com; p. 11 Peter Kniez/Shutterstock.com; p. 13 Roman Belogorodov/Shutterstock.com; p.15 Alizada Studios/Shutterstock.com; p.17 Jarlat Maletych/Shutterstock.com; p.19 Frolphy/Shutterstock.com; p.21 Avpics/Alamy.com; p.23 creativeneko/Shutterstock.com, (inset) Heydar Heydarov/Shutterstock.com; p.25 Sklo Studio/Shutterstock.com; p.27 Veyron Photo/Shutterstock.com; p.29 Yuri Kabantsev/Shutterstock.com.

Printed in the United States of America

CPSIA compliance information: Batch #CWENS23: For further information contact Enslow Publishing at 1-800-398-2504.

CONTENTS

Words in the glossary appear in **bold** type the first time they are used in the text.

The Porsche Name

The Porsche company was first founded in 1931. But its founder, Ferdinand Porsche, had already made a name for himself long before then. Ferdinand Porsche was an Austrian **engineer**. From the start of his career, his creative ideas led the way for car manufacturers around the world.

Over the years, Porsche cars have stood out for their **design**, speed, and style. They are some of the highest-priced cars on the market. That's because they're made with the greatest care and attention to even the smallest features.

The Porsche Semper Vivus was the first hybrid car.

Explore More!

Hybrid cars run on both gas and electricity. They're popular today because they're better for the planet than gas cars. Hybrids seem very modern, but did you know that Ferdinand Porsche designed the first-ever hybrid car way back in 1900?

Ferdinand Porsche

While working for Jacob Lohner, who worked for the Austrian royal court, Ferdinand Porsche designed the Lohner-Porsche. The Lohner-Porsche was an electric car. It only went about 35 miles (56.3 km) per hour, but it was the world's first all-wheel drive car. It also featured Porsche's invention, or creation: a wheel-hub engine. When Porsche showed the car at the 1900 World's Fair in Paris, France, it was a huge hit.

Porsche then worked for Austro-Daimler, an industrial company. While at Daimler, he moved to Stuttgart, Germany, in 1923. In 1931, Porsche started his own company in Stuttgart.

Explore More!

On September 19, 1909, Porsche's son, Ferdinand "Ferry" Porsche, was born. When he was old enough, Ferry started working at his father's car design company. Ferdinand Porsche died in 1951, and Ferry Porsche ran the company until his own death in 1998.

The 1900 Lohner-Porsche electric car is pictured here.

The Auto Union Racing Car

When Ferdinand Porsche first started his company, he didn't plan on building his own cars. Instead, he wanted to design cars for others. In 1933, Ferdinand and Ferry Porsche designed a grand prix race car for a company called Auto Union, which was formed from car companies Audi, Horch, Wanderer, and DKW.

The 1933 Auto Union car featured a 16-cylinder engine. Cylinders are what power a car's engine. The more cylinders a car has, the more powerful it is. The 16-cylinder Auto Union race car was a speed machine!

Grand prix refers to a series of international car races.

Explore More!

Porsche's Auto Union race car was different from other cars because its engine was placed in the back of the car instead of the front. This idea was later used in the Volkswagen Beetle, which Porsche also helped design.

Volkswagen

In 1934, Porsche was hired to create a "car for the people": the Volkswagen. Ferdinand and Ferry designed the Volkswagen Beetle. The Beetle's production was put on hold when World War II began in 1939.

During World War II, Porsche helped design German military cars, tanks, and aircraft. After the war ended, Ferdinand Porsche was put in prison for 20 months. It was during that time that Ferry Porsche and his sister Louise created the new Porsche company in Gmünd, Austria. Porsche shifted to producing its own cars instead of designing them for others.

The Beetle is one of the most successful car designs of all time.

Explore More!

In 1939, Porsche developed three racing coupes, or hard top, two door cars, called the Type 64. They were built for a high-speed road race from Berlin to Rome, but the race didn't happen. The Type 64s are the base of all Porsche sports cars.

The Gmünd Roadster

Ferry Porsche designed the first car to be built and sold by Porsche—the 356. He used the design and parts of the Volkswagen Beetle as a starting point, but wanted to create a lighter, faster car.

The 356 first hit the road on June 8, 1948. By the 1950s, it was one of the most popular cars on the market. People liked how easily the 356 handled. It was also faster and better-built than most other sports cars. Several different models of the 356 were produced from 1948 to 1965.

The 356 was nicknamed the Gmünd Roadster after the city where it was made.

Explore More!

The first 356 had a 1.1-liter, four-cylinder engine that produced 35 **horsepower** and could reach a top speed of 83 miles (133.6 km) per hour. The fastest 356 model was the Speedster. It could reach 112 miles (180.5 km) per hour.

The Popular Porsche 911

The Porsche 911 was introduced at the 1963 International Automobile Exhibition, or show, in Frankfurt, Germany. The first 911 was only available as a coupe and had a 2.0-liter, 6-cylinder engine that produced 130 horsepower.

Most sports cars of the day had four speeds. The 911 had five. It was also fast! The new engine allowed it to go from 0 to 60 miles (0 to 96.6 km) per hour in just nine seconds. The first Porsche 911 model was produced until 1989. Throughout the years, many different 911s have been made.

The 911 was originally named the 901.

Explore More!

The 911 did more than just replace the 356. It also outsold it! Today, the 911 is still Porsche's best-selling model of all time.

911 Race Cars

Ferdinand Porsche had a passion, or love, of race cars. He even raced some models himself. Over the years, Porsche has built not only **luxury** sports cars, but also some of the fastest race cars in the world.

Many of Porsche's most successful race cars were based on the 911. The 911 GT1, which was first produced in 1996, is one of the fastest cars Porsche has ever created. The Porsche 911 GT1 doesn't have much in common with the production model 911 you'd see on the road. It has a top speed of 193 miles (310.6 km) per hour.

The Porsche GT1 is considered a rare, or uncommon, supercar.

Explore More!

Porsche's race cars are different from its production models, or those sold to the public. Race cars are driven on special tracks, by special drivers, and have special parts and engines.

Porsche in Motorsport

Porsche makes race cars for different kinds of racing. In the past, Porsche has raced in Formula 1 races, but it has only one World Championship Grand Prix title, which dates back to the 1962 French Grand Prix.

Porsches have been successful in longer races though. The 24 Hours of Le Mans is the oldest **endurance** race in the world. Cars race for 24 hours. These cars have to be fast and run for a long time without breaking down. As of 2022, Porsche has won the 24 Hours of Le Mans 19 times.

The 911 RSR raced in Le Mans in 2019. It has a roll cage to keep the driver safe.

Car: 911 RSR
Engine: 4.2 liter (L)
Horsepower: 515 hp
Top Speed: 205 miles (330 km) per hour

Car: Porsche 911 GT3
Engine: 3.4L
Horsepower: 502 hp
Top Speed: 197 miles (317 km) per hour

Car: 2008 Porsche Boxster RS 60 Spyder
Engine: 3.4L
Horsepower: 303 hp
Top Speed: 170 miles (274 km) per hour

Explore More!

During their more than 60 years of taking part in motorsport, Porsche has had more than 30,000 race **victories** in many different categories, or groups. Their wins include 20 European mountain championships, and 11 Targa Florio, which is a road race in Sicily.

The Successful RS Spyder

Porsche introduced the RS Spyder in 1999. It won first place in its class in its first race at the 2005 American Le Mans Series. It won the ALMS LMP2 Championship three years in a row during the five years it raced.

The RS Spyder was named after Porsche's 550 Spyder of the 1950s. The 550 Spyder won the first race it **competed** in—the Nürburgring Eifel Race in 1953. Over its racing lifetime, the 550 Spyder raced in 370 races, took home 95 victories, and won its class 75 times.

The 1999 RS Spyder had 13 overall wins and 22 class wins.

Explore More!

The Porsche 550 Spyder was based on the Porsche 356. However, it was a roadster and didn't have the hard roof the 356 had. Porsche only produced 90 of the 550 Spyder, and 43 of them were built as nonracing customer cars.

The Boxster Roadster

In September 1996, Porsche introduced a new roadster. They named it the Boxster because of its engine's shape. The first generation of the Boxster, called the 986, had a powerful 2.5-liter, 6-cylinder engine. In 2000, the Boxster was built with a 2.7-liter, six-cylinder engine that produced 217 horsepower.

The base model 718 Boxster can go from 0 to 60 miles (0 to 96.6 km) per hour in just 4.9 seconds and has a top track speed of 170 miles (273.6 km) per hour. Its engine produces up to 300 horsepower.

Car buyers love the Boxster because of its classic look.

Explore More!

"Boxer" and "roadster" together make "Boxster." "Boxer" refers to the Boxster's engine type. A roadster is a car with two seats and a **convertible** roof.

The Fastback Coupe

In 2005, Porsche introduced a new car, which was based on the second and third generation Boxsters—the Cayman S. The Cayman offered Porsche drivers a more practical, or useful, version of the Boxster. Roadsters have limited trunk space. The Cayman offered a rear hatch, or door that opens up rather than out. This gives drivers more space to carry bags and other things.

The Cayman is a fastback coupe, which is a car with a roofline that slopes down at the back. The first Cayman had a 3.4-liter engine that produced 295 horsepower.

The 2014 Cayman, shown here, looked great and drove well!

Explore More!

A generation is a life cycle of a car's certain make and model.

A Crossover SUV

SUV is short for sport utility **vehicle**. These are bigger cars designed to fit more riders and their things. Porsche introduced the Cayenne in 2002. This was Porsche's first mid-size luxury crossover SUV.

The Cayenne seats up to five people. The Cayenne became the first Porsche to have an eight-cylinder, or V-8, engine since 1995. It's also the first production-model Porsche to have four doors. Even though the Cayenne is a larger car and can seat more passengers, it still has the common design elements of other Porsche models.

Special color options for the Cayenne include chalk and lava orange, shown below.

Explore More!

The Cayenne's first generation lasted until 2010. The second generation Cayennes, which came out in 2011, were also available as hybrids. Today, the Cayenne is in its third generation. The newest Cayenne's style looks more like a 911 than the earlier generations.

What's Next?

Today's Porsches are as speedy and stylish as ever. They also feature the newest **technology**. Buyers have many different models to choose from.

Electric and hybrid options are a key part of Porsche's current lineup. The 2022 Taycan is an electric sedan. The 2022 Panamera is available as a plug-in hybrid. The Macan SUV has been Porsche's most popular car since 2016. Porsche plans to offer an electric version of the Macan in 2024. In the years to come, Porsche promises to offer more **high-performance** electric and hybrid models.

Explore More!

One of the things that sets Porsches apart from other sports cars is that some have the **ignition** on the left side of the steering wheel. The left-side ignition means drivers can start the car while getting into it.

Porsches Today

Car: 2022
718 Boxster
Engine: 4.0L
Horsepower: 394 hp
Top Speed: about 170 miles (274 km) per hour

Car: 2022
Panamera 4S
Engine: 2.9L Twin Turbo V6
Horsepower: 443 hp
Top Speed: 183 miles (295 km) per hour

Car: 2022
Porsche 911
Engine: 3.0L Flat 6
Horsepower: 379 hp
Top Speed: 182 miles (293 km) per hour

Which Porsche do you like best?

GLOSSARY

compete: To try to win a contest with others.

convertible: A kind of car with a removable roof.

design: The pattern or shape of something. Also, to create the pattern or shape of something.

endurance: The power to do something hard for a long time.

engineer: Someone who plans and builds machines.

high-performance: Having to do with cars that are made for speed and power.

horsepower: The measure of power of a car's engine.

ignition: The car part that turns on the engine and starts the car.

luxury: Something that offers more than needed and is usually more expensive.

technology: Using science, engineering, and other industries to invent useful tools or to solve problems. Also a machine, piece of equipment, or method created by technology.

vehicle: An object that moves people from one place to another.

victories: Wins or successes.

FOR MORE INFORMATION

BOOKS

Mason, Paul. *Porsche, Audi, Mercedes*. New York, NY: PowerKids Press, 2019.

Rendle, Steve. *Race Cars*. New York, NY: Rosen Publishing Group, 2022.

Rendle, Steve. *Sports Cars*. New York, NY: Rosen Publishing Group, 2022.

WEBSITES

Porsche
www.porsche.com/usa/
Check out Porsche's current lineup!

Stuttcars
www.stuttcars.com/ferdinand-porsche/
Read more about Ferdinand Porsche, founder of Porsche.

24H Le Mans
www.24h-lemans.com/en
Learn more about 24 Hours of Le Mans racing.

Publisher's note to educators and parents: Our editors have carefully reviewed these websites to ensure that they are suitable for students. Many websites change frequently, however, and we cannot guarantee that a site's future contents will continue to meet our high standards of quality and educational value. Be advised that students should be closely supervised whenever they access the internet.

INDEX